W9-BAK-172

THE STORY BEHIND

COTTON

Heidi Moore

Heinemann Library
Chicago, Illinois

Edited by Louise Galpine, David Andrews, and Diyan Leake
Designed by Philippa Jenkins and Artistix
Original illustrations © Capstone Global Library, LLC 2009
Illustrated by Gary Slater/Specs Art
Picture research by Mica Brancic and Elaine Willis
Originated by Modern Age Repro House Ltd
Printed in China by CTPS

13 12 11 10 09
10 9 8 7 6 5 4 3 2 1

Library of Congress Cataloging-in-Publication Data
Moore, Heidi, 1976-
The story behind cotton / Heidi Moore.
p. cm. -- (True stories)
Includes bibliographical references and index.
ISBN 978-1-4329-2341-9 (hc)
1. Cotton--Juvenile literature. I. Title.
SB249.M58 2008
633.5'1--dc22

Acknowledgments
The author and publishers are grateful to the following for permission to reproduce copyright material: Alamy pp. **6** (© Inga Spence), **8** (© dbimages), **15** (© Dinodia Images), **24** (© Stuart Kelly); Art Archive p. **10** (© Mireille Vautier); © Corbis p. **5**; Corbis pp. **14** (© Bettmann), **18** (© Bettmann), **20** (ClassicStock/© H. Armstrong Roberts), **25** (© Wally McNamee); Getty Images p. **4** (The Image Bank/© Joe Schmeizer); http://memory.loc.gov/ammem/snhtml/snhome.html p. **19**; © Mary Evans Picture Library 2008 pp. **12**, 13; © Photolibrary.com 2008 p. **21** (Index Stock Imagery); Photolibrary.com p. **22** (© Paul Nevin); Science Photo Library p. **9** (AG Stock USA/© Bill Barksdale), **23** (© Victor De Schwanberg), **26** (Eurelios/© Phillipe Plailly); Shutterstock p. **iii** (©Wendy Perry); www.transfair.org p. **24**; © The Bridgeman Art Library p. **16** (Yale Center for British Art, Paul Mellon Collection, USA).

Cover photograph of a cotton boll reproduced with permission of Photolibrary Group (Animals Animals/ Richard Shiell).

Contents

Some words are shown in bold, **like this**. You can find out what they mean by looking in the glossary.

A Cotton Tale

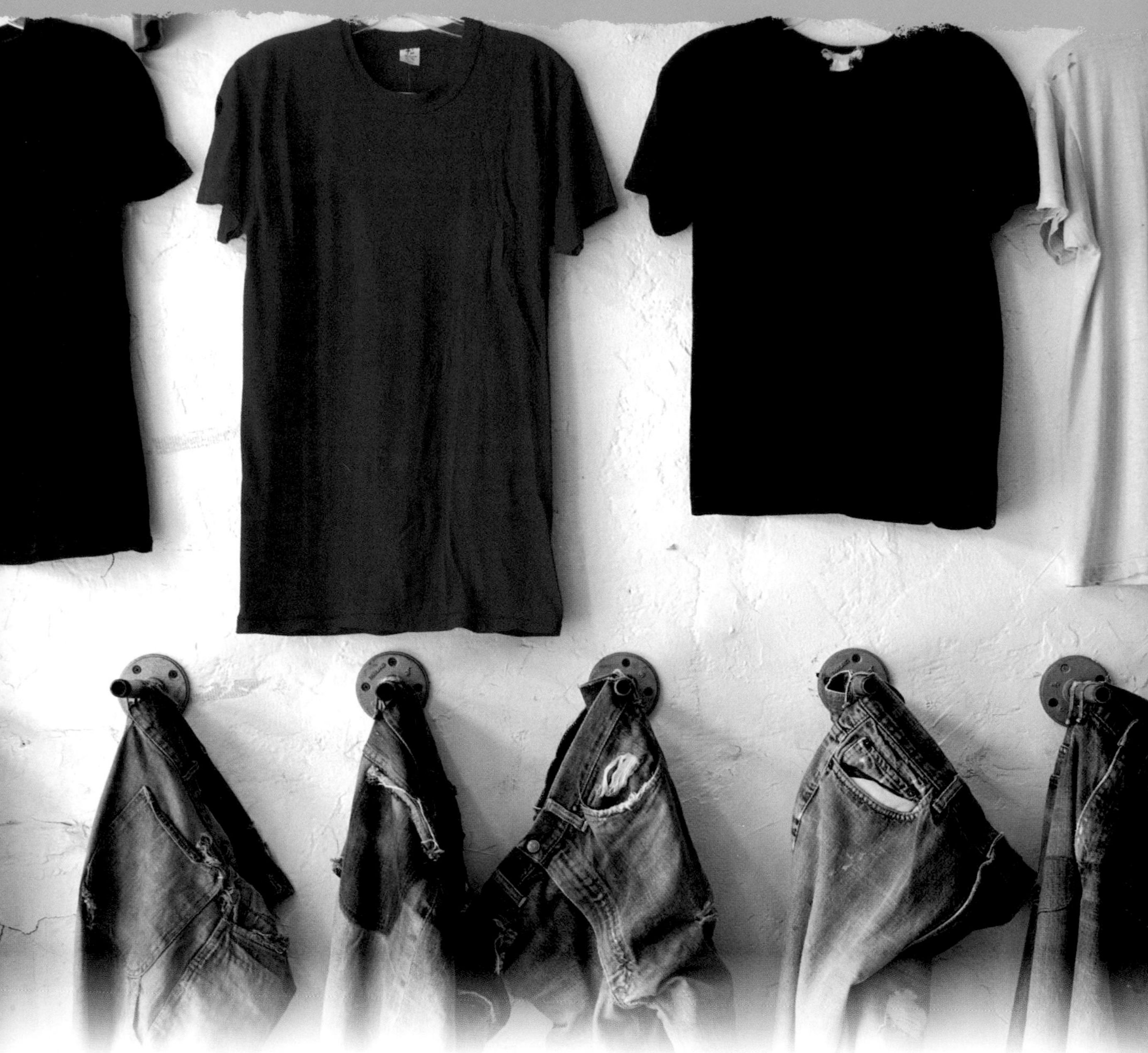

▲ **Cotton is part of many of the things we wear every day.**

Have you used cotton today? Chances are, you have probably used cotton in some form. In fact, you might have used it more than once.

Think about your day so far. Did you wake up in a bed with cotton sheets? Did you dry your hands on a cotton towel? Did you put on a T-shirt or jeans made from cotton? Did you use cotton balls or cotton pads?

An important plant

Cotton is everywhere. It is used to make many of the goods we come across every day.

Cotton is a plant that grows widely. It is easy to work with and is used to make many affordable products, ranging from clothes to cooking oil. These factors have made cotton one of the most important **crops** in the world. (Crops are plants that are grown in order to be sold.)

But did you know that cotton has grown on Earth for more than 5,000 years? Ancient peoples made rich **textiles** (cloths) from cotton thousands of years ago. Cotton also played a key role in **slavery**. There is much more to the history of cotton than you might have thought. Read on to learn the true story of cotton ...

Did you know? 

One **bale** (a large, tightly pressed bundle) of cotton weighs 217.7 kilograms (480 pounds). That amount of cotton makes:

215 pairs of jeans
249 bed sheets
690 bath towels
1,217 T-shirts
1,256 pillowcases
3,085 diapers
4,321 socks
313,600 $100 bills

▼ Cotton grows in fluffy white balls.

Planting the Seed

▲ **Cotton blossoms start out as white flowers. Then they turn red.**

Cotton grows in warm areas all over the world. It needs about 150 to 200 days without frost to grow.

The cottonseed is planted in spring or the beginning of the growing season. In two months, the plant grows to about 30 centimeters (1 foot) high. Then, 80 to 100 days after planting, white blossoms form on the plants. The blossoms turn red overnight, then fall off.

Growing fibers

Each blossom leaves behind a small, green pod with seeds in it. This seedpod grows for about 55 to 80 days. During this time, the seeds inside the pod grow hairs, or **fibers**, that attach to the pod. The pod grows larger as more and more fibers form inside it.

Finally, when the seedpod is ripe, it bursts into a fluffy white ball. This white ball is called the **boll**. At that point the fibers are still attached to the seed. (Another word for cotton fiber is **lint**.) The fibers are the most important part of the cotton plant. They will be **harvested** (picked and gathered) to make cotton thread and cloth. The ripe boll with fibers and seeds attached is called seed cotton.

The ripe bolls are harvested by hand or by machine. A mature (grown) cotton plant can be 0.6 to 1.5 meters (2 to 5 feet) in height.

Fine cotton 

The length of a cotton fiber is called its staple. The longer the staple, the finer the cotton is.

▼ **This picture shows how a cotton boll looks when it is sliced across the middle.**

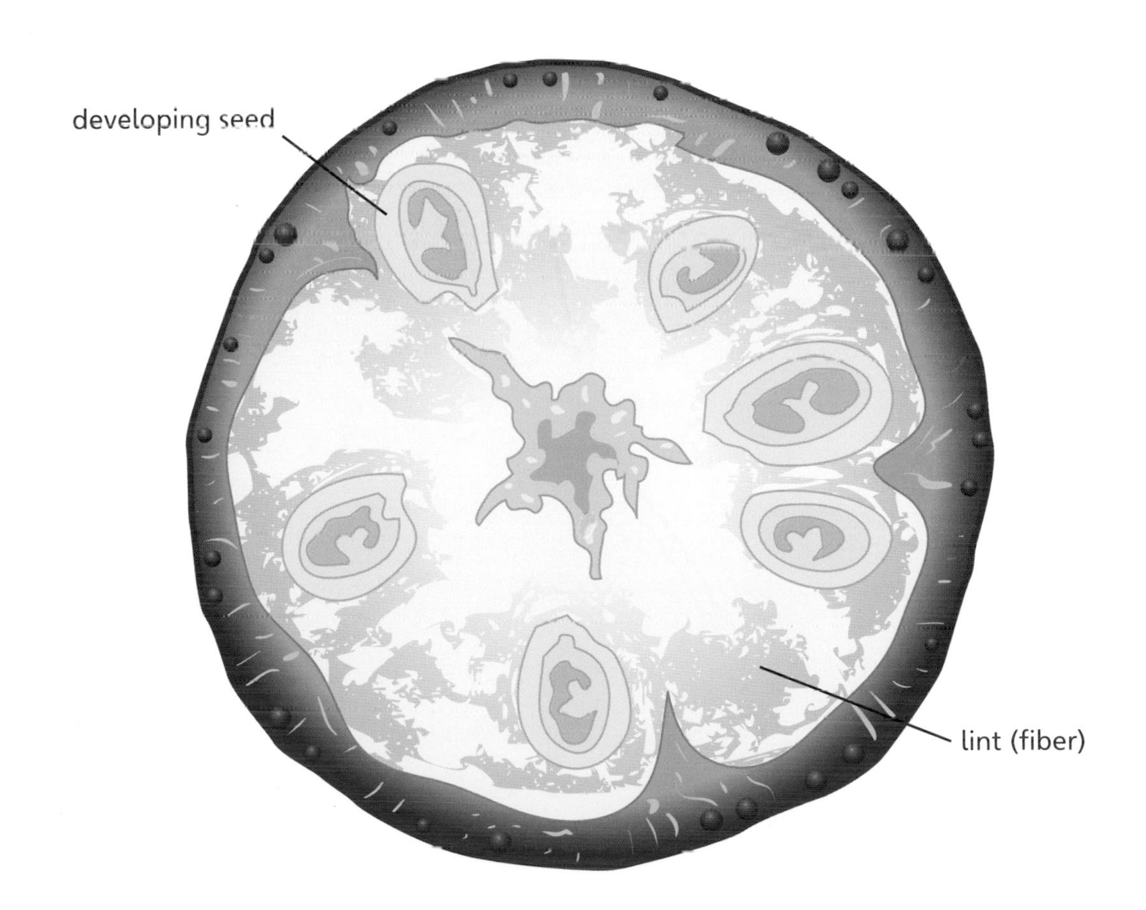

Uses of cotton

All parts of the cotton plant are useful. The hard outside part of the cottonseed is the hull. Hulls are used to feed farm animals and to enrich soil. The stalks or leaves are plowed into the ground, also to enrich soil.

Long cotton fibers are used to make cloth and cotton clothing. These strong fibers make cotton clothing very durable (long lasting). Short fibers called linters are used in making paper, mattress stuffing, cushions, cotton pads, explosives, and other products.

Cotton for clothing

Cotton has a long journey from the farm to your closet. First it must be harvested. Then the lint must be separated from the seeds. Finally the cotton is cleaned, dried, and formed into **bales**.

In northern China, people wear padded cotton coats. They add more layers as it gets colder. They say it is "two-coat weather" or "three-coat weather."

Bales of cotton are then sold to **textile** makers, who operate textile **mills** (factories where machines are used to make goods from natural materials). At the mill the cotton is spun into thread or yarn. Then the thread or yarn is knitted or woven into cloth.

This last step is often done by loom. A loom is a frame-like machine that laces together two or more sets of threads or yarn to make cloth. People have used simple looms for thousands of years.

Cottonseed oil

Cotton is also used for other kinds of products. Cottonseeds are pressed to make cottonseed oil. This is used for cooking and for making margarine. The oil is also used to make soap, medicine, and makeup.

▼ **This huge pile of cottonseeds is ready to be pressed into oil.**

Cotton's History

▲ **This picture shows an Aztec woman weaving cotton.**

Cotton is an ancient plant. The first wild cotton plants appeared on Earth 7 million years ago. About 5,500 years ago, people began to weave cotton fabric.

The oldest known pieces of cotton thread and cloth date from 3000 BCE. They were found in the Indus River Valley region. Today the region is part of the countries of Pakistan and India.

5,000 to 5,500 years ago

Cotton farming and textile weaving begins in the Indus River Valley.

2500 BCE

People in what is now Peru make fishing nets from cotton.

6000 BCE | 5000 BCE | 4000 BCE | 3000 BCE

Evidence from fossils (remains of living things found in soil) shows that cotton plants also grew in an area that is now part of Mexico as early as 2900 BCE. By 1900 BCE people in Central and South America were weaving **textiles** from cotton.

Arab traders brought cotton to Europe around 700 CE. By 1000 CE cotton had spread across Europe through trading. People everywhere were amazed by this lightweight fabric with so many uses.

What's in a name? 

The word *cotton* comes from the Arab word *qutun* or *kutun*, meaning "textile."

The Italian explorer Christopher Columbus came across cotton on his journey to the Americas. On October 12, 1492, Columbus wrote, "Afterwards they [the Arawak people of the Bahamas] came swimming to the boats, bringing parrots, balls of cotton thread ... and many other things, which they exchanged for articles [objects] we gave them, such as glass beads."

Cotton as money 

Cotton has been used as money for a long time. The Aztecs, who lived from about 1250 to 1550 in what is now Mexico, used cotton cloth as payment. Today, cotton is used to make paper bills.

1900 BCE People begin weaving cloth from cotton.

700 CE Arab traders bring cotton to Europe.

1000 Cotton is found across Europe.

1250–1550 The Aztecs use cotton cloth as money.

2000 BCE | 1000 BCE | 0 | 1000 CE | 2000

▲ The spinning jenny could spin sixteen threads at once.

Britain's textile boom

By the 1600s, cotton textiles were a major **industry** (type of business) in Great Britain. Textile **mills** had a hard time keeping up with demand. But a wave of exciting new inventions in the 1700s changed that.

The Industrial Revolution

These changes in cotton production helped start the **Industrial Revolution**. This took place in England between 1760 and 1815. It was a time of widespread changes, with machines taking over work that was once done by hand. These changes spread to the United States, Europe, and across the world.

1600s
Cotton textiles are a major industry in Great Britain.

1733
British inventor John Kay creates the flying shuttle.

1600

1700

The flying shuttle

Invented in: 1733
Inventor: John Kay
This device was a weaving machine. Weaving by machine was much faster than weaving by hand. Now textile mills could produce much more cloth.

The spinning jenny

Invented in: 1764
Inventor: James Hargreaves
This device spun a number of threads at once. Spinners could then make yarn very quickly.

The water frame

Invented in: 1769
Inventor: Richard Arkwright
This new weaving machine ran on water power. It made spinning cotton yarn faster than ever before.

The spinning mule

Invented in: 1779
Inventor: Samuel Crompton
This amazing device let workers spin 1,000 threads at once. It could produce fine or coarse (rough) thread.

Factories got bigger during the Industrial Revolution and cotton mills could produce more textiles.

1760–1815
The Industrial Revolution takes place in Great Britain, then spreads to the United States and other countries.

1764
British inventor James Hargreaves develops the spinning jenny.

1769
British inventor Richard Arkwright invents the water frame.

1800

▲ Children worked long hours for very little pay in mills all over the United States. This stopped in 1938 when fair labor laws came in.

"The Oldham Weaver" 

An 1815 poem called "The Oldham Weaver" is about life in a textile mill in northern England. The first line says, "Oh, I'm a poor cotton weaver, as many a one knows. I've nowt [nothing] for to eat, and I've worn out my clothes."

New machines, new problems

These inventions made it faster and cheaper to make cotton yarn and cloth. But there were not enough adult workers to run the new machines. So, many children were sent to work at the mills.

The mills were often terrible places. People worked 12 to 13 hours a day, 6 days a week, for little pay. Children got hurt when their clothes caught in the machines. Sometimes their fingers got caught and were cut off.

Cotton and Gandhi

From 1858 to 1947, Great Britain ruled India. India supplied raw cotton to Britain, where it was spun into cloth. The British then sold the cloth very cheaply in India. This was unfair to Indian weavers, who could not produce such cheap cloth. This angered the people of India. Many Indians were experts at weaving cotton. They wanted to make cloth in their own country, not buy it from Britain.

The Indian leader Mahatma Gandhi spoke out against British rule. He told the people of his country to buy only textiles made in India. Gandhi himself was an expert cotton spinner. He once said, "With every thread I draw, I am spinning the destiny [future] of India."

Say it in Hindi 

The cotton-related words *calico*, *dungaree*, *khaki*, *sash*, and *pajamas* all come from Hindi. Hindi is one of the languages spoken in India.

▼ **Gandhi believed that Indians should go back to weaving cotton. He often took his spinning wheel with him. when he traveled.**

Cotton in the New World

▲ **In the 1700s, cotton was sent by ship from the United States to be woven into cloth in mills in Great Britain.**

The American **colonies** began growing cotton in the 1600s. This land was ruled by Great Britain. By the late 1700s, after the colonies gained independence from Britain, cotton was a major **crop** in the United States. The United States grew cotton to ship to Britain, where it was made into cloth.

In 1793 an American named Eli Whitney invented the cotton **gin**. This device could quickly separate the cotton **fibers** from the seeds. The new machine could do the work of 50 people!

1600s
The American colonies begin growing cotton.

1776
The United States claims independence from Great Britain with the Declaration of Independence.

1600 1700

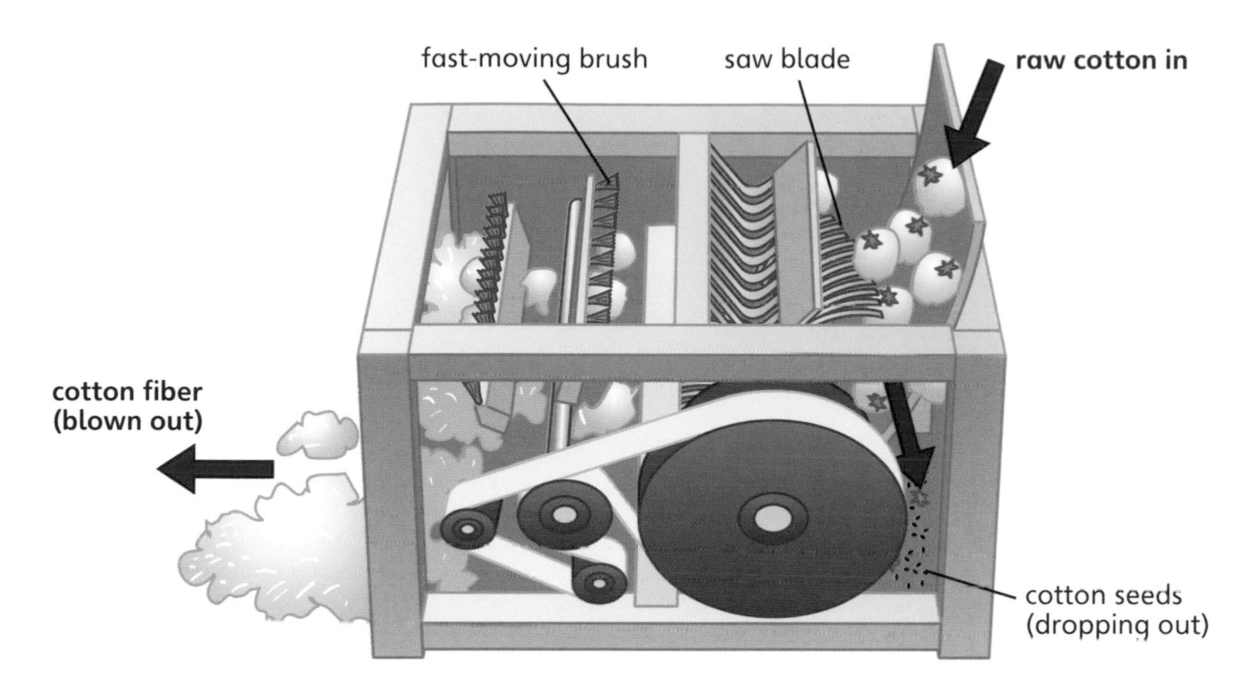

▲ **The cotton gin could quickly separate the cotton fibers from the seeds.**

Slavery

Cotton then became the most important crop in the United States. But it went hand in hand with the terrible practice of **slavery**. Owners of large cotton farms called plantations needed workers to plant and pick cotton, as well as other crops. So, they turned to slavery.

Thousands of people were taken against their will from their homes in Africa and the Caribbean. They were brought to the Americas on large slave ships. Many died on the journey from illness or lack of food. Those who made it to the Americas faced lives of hard labor with little chance of escape.

"It was work hard, get beatings and half fed . . . The times I hated most was picking cotton when the frost was on the **bolls**. My hands get sore and crack open and bleed."

Mary Reynolds, former enslaved person, speaking in 1937 at age 105

Enslaving millions 

In 1790 there were about 650,000 slaves in the United States. By 1850 there were 3.2 million. More than half of them worked on cotton farms.

1793
U.S. inventor Eli Whitney invents the cotton gin; this leads to a cotton boom in the United States, as well as the rise of slavery.

1850
Millions of slaves work on cotton fields in the southern United States.

1800 1900

▲ This drawing shows slaves using a cotton gin.

"King Cotton"

Over time many Americans began to disagree with slavery. They learned of the harsh conditions and beatings many enslaved people faced. People in the Northern states wanted to end the brutal practice. But people in the Southern states believed they had the right to own slaves. They believed their wealth depended on slavery.

In 1858 a Southern politician named James Henry Hammond spoke out about cotton: "You dare not make war on cotton! No power on Earth dares make war upon it. Cotton is king!"

He was wrong. The United States went to war over slavery. This **Civil War** lasted from 1861 to 1865. Nearly one million people lost their lives fighting, including many former slaves.

1861–65
During the U.S. Civil War, the North and South battle over slavery.

1860 1865

A new system

When the North won the war, nearly 4 million former slaves were freed. But it was difficult for many to find jobs. Many had not been to school and had few skills other than farming.

A new system of sharecropping arose. In this system, land owners let farmers use a plot of land in return for a share of the crop. This was better than slavery, but it was still unfair. Many were in debt to the land owner forever. Sharecroppers worked long hours for little pay.

▼ Sylvia Cannon, a former enslaved person, spoke in 1937 at age 85, about how some things were worse after the end of slavery.

Code No.
Project, 1885-(1)
Prepared by Annie Ruth Davis
Place, Marion, S.C.
Date, October 5, 1937

No. Words ________
Reduced from ____ words
Rewritten by
____
Page 6.

185

old Massa. Den if I get sick, I call on it en somebody come. Wouldn' take nothin for it, honey."

"Times was sho better long time ago den dey be now. I know it. Yes,mam, I here frettin myself to death after dem dat gone. Colored people never had no debt to pay in slavery time. **Never hear tell bout no colored people been put in jail fore freedom. Had more to eat en more to wear den en had good clothes all de time cause white folks furnish everything, everything.** Dat is, had plenty to eat such as we had. Had plenty peas en rice en hog meat en rabbit en fish en such as dat. Colored people sho fare better in slavery time be dat de white folks had to look out for dem. Had dey extra crop what dey had time off to work every Saturday. White folks tell dem what dey

The Jeans Craze

▲ **This photo from the 1890s shows factory workers wearing jeans for work.**

Today almost everyone wears jeans. But jeans started out as work pants for farmers, miners, and factory workers. They were designed to be tough and long lasting. Before jeans came along, work pants often ripped at the seams.

Around 1870 a U.S. tailor named Jacob Davis added metal fasteners called rivets to work pants. This kept them from ripping. Soon Davis could not keep up with the demand for his work pants with rivets. So, he wrote a letter to a U.S. businessman named Levi Strauss. Davis asked for money to help patent his product. A patent gives someone the right to produce something for a period of time.

Blue jeans

Strauss and Davis went into business together to make jeans. The most popular fabric was denim (see box below) dyed indigo, or blue. Levi Strauss & Company became known for its blue jeans.

Today people around the world wear jeans. They come in many different colors and styles. Their prices have gone way up, too. What would the miners and farmers of the early 1900s think of $200 jeans?

Denim from France? 

The word *denim* comes from the French term *serge de Nîmes*. *Serge de Nîmes* is a silk and wool blend. It is very different from the tough cotton cloth used to make jeans. But both materials are woven on an angle, not straight across. When U.S. clothing makers needed a name for indigo cotton cloth, they dropped the first word and combined the last two to form *denim*.

▼ **Jeans today are more about style than work.**

Cotton Today

▲ **This airplane is spraying chemicals over cotton fields.**

Cotton is still a very important **crop** today. In 2007 alone, people around the world used 24.4 metric tons (26.9 million tons) of cotton. Cotton grows in more than 100 countries.

Cotton farms take up a lot of land, so they have a big impact on the planet. Many cotton farmers use chemicals called **pesticides** to fight cotton pests. In the past, insects such as the **boll** weevil, pink bollworm, and cotton leafworm destroyed many cotton fields. People began using chemical pesticides in the early 1900s to save plants from these pests. Today 25 percent of all pesticides used worldwide are used in growing cotton.

Problems with pesticides

These pesticides have a serious effect on the planet. They kill all insects, not just harmful ones. They pollute (dirty) the ground and water sources, spreading far beyond the cotton field. Pesticides can harm people and animals. Scientists still are not certain what long-term effects years of pesticide use will have on Earth.

Today some farmers are growing cotton a different way. They use organic, or natural, farming methods that have been in use for hundreds of years. Organic farmers fertilize (enrich) the soil with manure (animal waste) and fight pests safely without harmful chemicals. When buying cotton products, be sure to look for a label that says "certified organic." This means they are guaranteed to be organic.

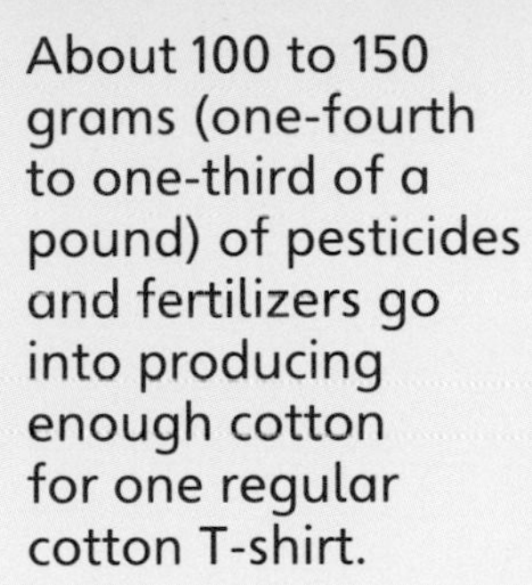

What's in your T-shirt?

About 100 to 150 grams (one-fourth to one-third of a pound) of pesticides and fertilizers go into producing enough cotton for one regular cotton T-shirt.

▼ **These labels show that a product is made with organic cotton.**

▲ **Look for the Fair Trade label when buying cotton clothing.**

Fair trade cotton

Many people are concerned about how cotton products are made. Some people making cotton clothing work in sweatshops. Sweatshops are dangerous places where people work long hours for little pay.

The United States and Britain have laws to make sure people in their countries are paid and treated fairly. But some countries do not have laws like this, or factory owners in those countries do not follow the laws that are in place. Plus, there are no laws in the United States or Britain that make sure that goods sold there were produced fairly in other countries.

Today China is the world's top cotton producer. However, some people in China work in sweatshop conditions. Some people believe goods should not be bought from China until working conditions improve.

Top five growers

The top cotton producers today are:

China	5.5 million metric tons (6.1 million tons) per year
United States	4.7 million metric tons (5.2 million tons) per year
India	2.7 million metric tons (2.5 million tons) per year
Pakistan	2.4 million metric tons (2.2 million tons) per year
Uzbekistan	1.1 million metric tons (1.2 million tons) per year

One thing people can do is to buy "**fair trade**" products. Fair trade products are produced by workers who are paid and treated fairly. Right now only products such as coffee and tea are Fair Trade Certified in the United States. But in Britain and Europe people can buy Fair Trade Certified clothing and cotton products.

▼ These people are making cotton goods in a cramped sweatshop with no windows in Phnom Penh, Cambodia.

This scientist is working with genetically modified cotton plants in India.

The future of cotton

The cotton plant is different today than it was 5,000 years ago. Over time it has slowly changed. Recently, modern science has sped up the rate of change.

Scientists have created **genetically modified**, or GM, cotton. Each **gene** in a living thing contains code that that controls how a part of the living thing looks or acts. With GM cotton, these genes are modified, or changed. Scientists replace some of the genes in cotton plants with genes for a type of insect poison. These genes make the plants resistant to certain insects. GM cotton also produces more cotton per **harvest**.

There can be problems with GM plants. No one is quite sure how these plants affect non-GM plants nearby. Some worry that GM plants may not be safe to eat. (Remember that cottonseed oil is in many things people eat.)

GM labels

Some countries, such as Britain, label products that are genetically modified. Then buyers can decide for themselves whether they want to buy them.

Stronger pests

In 1996 scientists created GM cotton that could make its own bollworm poison. For about 10 years, the plant was a success. It resisted the bollworm.

Then something strange happened. The bollworms began to get stronger. Now they are no longer harmed by the poison. In trying to combat the pest, scientists made it stronger and harder to kill!

What's to come?

The future of cotton may bring other exciting new changes. But one thing is likely never to change. Cotton will always be an important part of our daily lives.

Timeline

(These dates are often approximations.)

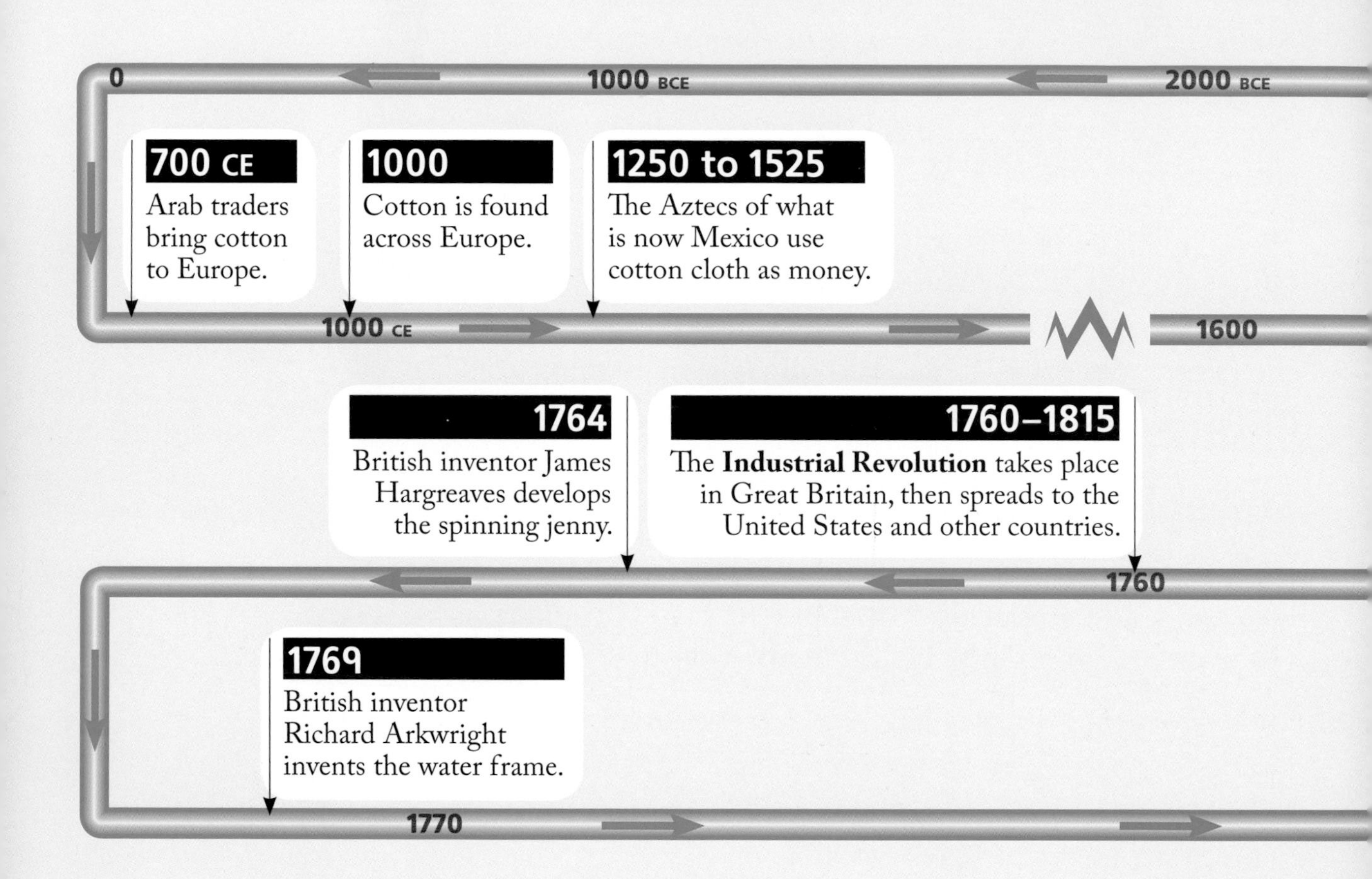

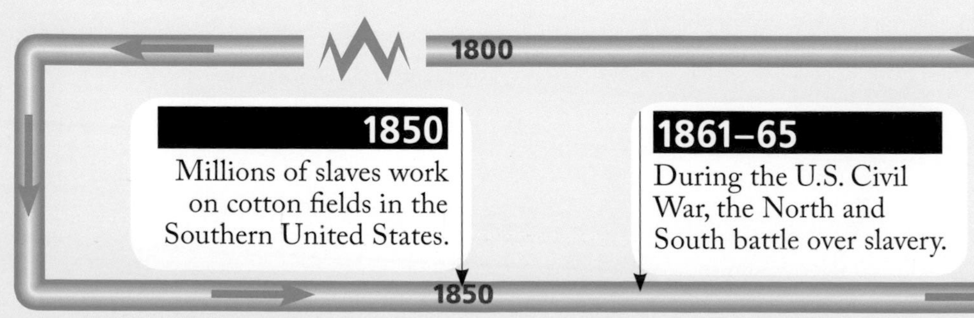

This symbol shows where there is a change of scale in the timeline, or where a long period of time with no noted events has been left out.

5,000 to 5,500 years ago
Cotton farming and **textile** weaving begins in the Indus River Valley.

6000 BCE
5000 BCE

2500 BCE
People in what is now Peru make fishing nets from cotton.

3000 BCE
4000 BCE

1600s
Cotton textiles are a major **industry** in Great Britain. The American **colonies** begin growing cotton.

1733
British inventor John Kay creates the flying shuttle.

1700
1750

1776
The United States claims independence from Great Britain with the Declaration of Independence.

1779
British inventor Samuel Crompton develops the spinning mule.

1780

1793
U.S. inventor Eli Whitney invents the cotton **gin**; this leads to a cotton boom in the United States, as well as the rise of **slavery**.

1790

early 1900s
The use of **pesticides** begins.

2007
People around the world use 24.4 metric tons (26.9 million tons) of cotton; 25 percent of all pesticides are used each year in growing cotton.

1900
2000

Glossary

bale large, tightly pressed bundle. After cotton is picked, it is packed into bales.

BCE meaning "before the common era." When this appears after a date, it refers to the time before the Christian religion began. BCE dates are always counted backwards.

boll fluffy white ball of ripe cotton. Cotton bolls are harvested by hand or by machine.

CE meaning "common era." When this appears after a date, it refers to the time after the Christian religion began.

civil war war between people of the same country

colony land ruled by another land far away. The United States was once a British colony.

crop plant that is grown to be sold. Cotton is an important crop in many countries.

fair trade food, clothing, or other product made by people who are treated fairly and paid a fair wage. If people buy fair trade products, they know that the people who made them were treated fairly.

fiber long, thin natural structure that can be spun into thread. Cotton is prized for its soft but strong fibers.

gene code in the cells of a living thing that controls how a part of the living thing looks or acts. Scientists can replace genes in plants and animals.

genetically modified (GM) food or product that contains changed code. Scientists are not sure about the effects of genetically modified plants.

gin machine that quickly separates cotton fibers from the seeds. U.S. inventor Eli Whitney invented the cotton gin in 1793.

harvest time for picking or gathering crops; also, to pick or gather crops. When the cotton is ripe, it is time to harvest it.

Industrial Revolution time of widespread changes in Great Britain, the United States, and Europe roughly between 1760 and 1815, during which machines took over work that was once done by hand. Many machines for cotton production were created during the Industrial Revolution.

industry type of work or business. The cotton industry has been an important source of wealth for many countries.

lint cotton fiber. Cotton thread is made from the lint.

mill factory where machines are used to make goods from natural materials. Cotton mills made it easier and faster to make cotton cloth.

pesticide chemical that kills pests. Pesticides kill pests, but they may harm other insects and animals.

slavery system in which humans own other humans. Slavery ended in the United States in 1865.

textile cloth. The Aztecs made fine cotton textiles.

Find Out More

Books

Gunderson, Jessica. *Eli Whitney and the Cotton Gin*. Mankato, Minn.: Capstone, 2007.

Masters, Nancy Robinson. *Inventions That Shaped the World: The Cotton Gin*. New York: Franklin Watts, 2006.

Nelson, Robin. *From Cotton to T-Shirt (Start to Finish)*. Minneapolis: Lerner, 2003.

Websites

Learn about the early history of cotton.
www.historyforkids.org/learn/clothing/cotton.htm

Read about cotton production, from the farm to the textile mill.
www.cottonsjourney.com/Storyofcotton/

Play a game to become a cotton millionaire in Great Britain in the 1800s.
www.bbc.co.uk/history/british/victorians/launch_gsms_cotton_millionaire.shtml

Places to visit

The Cotton Museum at the Memphis Cotton Exchange
65 Union Avenue
Memphis, Tennessee 38103

Learn the story of the cotton industry in the state of Tennessee and see how cotton affected daily life in the South.

Louisiana State Cotton Museum
7162 Highway 65 North
Lake Providence, Louisiana 71254

This museum explores the history of cotton in Louisiana. Crank a real cotton gin in the gin building. Visit a planter's house that is 100 years old, a sharecropper's cabin, and a plantation church.